# POEMS ETCETERA FOR ALL

J E Dennis

MINERVA PRESS
LONDON
MIAMI   RIO DE JANEIRO   DELHI

ISBN  0  75411  519  4


First Published 2001 by
MINERVA PRESS
315–317 Regent Street
London W1R 7YB


Printed in Great Britain for Minerva Press

POEMS ETCETERA FOR ALL

*With many thanks to*
*Beatrice Walton, Stephen Finch,*
*Kevin Fallon and Harold Huson*


Church House Nursing Home
Coole Lane
Austerson
Nantwich
Cheshire CW5 8AB
England

## Contents

## A Pet

A pet is what we have at home;
Sits by the fire, will never roam;
Some will bark, some meow,
Some will make a sound somehow.

Some pets know their master's voice;
Where there's one, there is no choice;
He's always comfy in his bed,
Will always come, if he's fed.

Sometimes he wanders far from home
So he's lost, so asks a bobby;
Way home is found again by boys in blue;
Will make his way about, his hobby.

Sometimes a pet has many more
To show how popular she's become;
The shops help with increasing birth
Now that she's become a mum.

A pet will stick by you for life,
So show him that you really care,
He never lets stray hands go near you;
Burglars too – they must beware.

## *Let's Travel*

I guess I've travelled round the world,
Seen the flags of nations furled
And waterfall swept from the sky;
Don't know who made them quite so high.

Seen you the tigers of Bengal
They make all others seem so small;
The elephant is pride of all,
Though quite massive, is not so tall.

Zebras, striped right round their girth
And bound then to cause a lot of mirth;
The spiders, though not great in size,
Are bound to cause the most surprise.

The pumas and the cheetah, too,
Not all are found inside a zoo;
One thing links us, you will see,
That's if you travel by the sea.

Things are just not what they seem
Because you've seen things in a dream;
When you've been and seen the rest
You will agree that we're the best.

## *Autumn*

The colours change and they will show
Resemblance to our own rainbow;
The trees once were a shade of green,
But now they have a different sheen.

The sun helps grow each budding flower
And each shares the autumn flower;
Each day increases by degrees
To help the growth of leaves on trees.

Our autumn gently starts to show
That winter leads us on to snow;
This spreads our garden with hygiene
And leaves it looking nice and clean.

The flowers need a lot of work,
Work from which we do not shirk;
We carefully put the seeds in place;
When they start growing, see our face.

In autumn our mistakes are buried from sight,
Though we strove to get things right;
Next year we hope we're on the ball
And our daises grow quite tall.

## A Thousand Ages

A thousand ages, so we are told,
Are like an evening gone,
But we don't think so far ahead,
Though troubles we have none.

But we think back, as best we can
On what has troubled us
But try as we might, we cannot find
What has caused the fuss.

We may have changed our state of mind,
Forgive us, we do,
And as we judge each one is good,
Make sure that one is you.

We find that this old earth of ours
Is round as it can be,
And people from another world
Are just like you and me.

So there we have the same old world
The same as it began
So if we try at any age
It's not too late for fun.

## *I Want To Be a Sportsman*

I have dreamed of being a sportsman
Since I was quite a lad;
I kicked the winning FA Cup goal,
At fourteen that's not bad!

A referee appealed to me,
We could sort out disastrous scores;
A match could be played within all the rules,
And no player would need have sores.

An asset would be a long stayer
Who thought of the club as his home,
No matter how good the incentive,
He decided never to roam.

He decided he never would tackle,
Except in the nicest of ways,
And so, in the game, he earned the good name
That would last to the end of his days.

And so he became a great sportsman
With all the advantage of fame;
When asked for tips he smilingly said,
'You must always play the game.'

## No Room at the Inn

'Sorry we've no room today,'
The landlord cried above the din,
'The stable is the only room.'
He thought, and let them in.

The place was dark and dismal;
The animals thought it great,
But Mary had to make it nice,
Which they'd appreciate.

The stable had a brushout,
The crib turned into a bed,
So when at last the night-time came
Our Jesus laid his head.

The three kings travelled by the stars,
Which led them on their way;
And they held their baby son,
And this quite made their day.

All this, two thousand years ago,
The rest you know quite well,
How Jesus taught us to avoid
That fearsome place called Hell.

## Noah and his Ark

As Noah said when in the Ark,
'This one will do for me;
After tests it looks as though
We're off, across the sea.'

So as they crowded all around
To hear our Noah's view,
'Of course I'll take you all with me,
But you must come two by two.'

A lion soon found a running mate,
A seal found one to match,
In fact, all who sailed upon the Ark
Had one mate in the batch.

They sailed away for many a day;
Doves flew and looked out for the land.
This came in view and that's when they knew
That this is what they'd planned.

Noah landed the Ark when land was in sight;
The trip had been lots of fun,
But he knew in his heart that he must make a start
On his new life just begun.

## A Baby's Smile

A baby's smile
Makes life worthwhile,
Especially if he is of you;
He smiles all around
Until he has found
His mother,
Who looks just like you.
He smiles at his best
(Though he dislikes the rest)
Until you have come into view.
He will then raise his arm
To attract all your charm
Because, Mum, he really loves you.
So this baby of mine
Gets old in his time
As we, in our time
Will do, too.
So whatever the age
Our love-child may reach,
He always has memories
Of you.

## *Si j'étais roi* (*If I were king*)

If I were king, I'd make a list
Of things I'd like to do;
I'd abolish income tax,
I'm sure it would please you.

There are so many other things
With which you disagree,
Perhaps get rid of all of them
And start again you see.

No rubbish to confront us,
The bin it is not there,
The smoke alarm is missing
Of this you must beware.

We must learn that giving up
Will put us in the mire,
For who will come to fetch our bins?
Or who'll put out a fire?

Can we ever be contented
With what little we have got?
Or can we keep improving things?
Can we? Or can we not?

## Is There Room?

Oh, is there any room for me?
The lonely crocus cried;
The daffodils had spread right out,
I looked and almost died.

It was indeed a forest
That slowly came to view,
The daffodils looked everywhere
To show their buds anew.

But nature has its own way
To ration all the ground,
So daffs may come and daffs may go
Then crocuses abound.

The colours will astound you
As you gently walk around.
The bulbs you planted innocently
Now occupy the ground.

Give thanks to all who please you,
Wait months to make it so,
And they appear to brighten us
In rain or in the snow.

## *Fellow Workers of Church House*

We thank you, fellow workers,
Whatever is your name,
If it wasn't for your efforts,
We'd never be the same.

The work they do must surely wear them down,
Yet they will smile and try to sing
Despite the odds
And never wear a frown.

We see them in the morning
As we begin the day,
But they arose some hours before
To begin their roundelay.

They help us in the dining room
And help us to our seat;
They say they're pleased to see us,
Especially when we eat.

So, for a change, let's give our thanks;
How lucky we all are,
For when we most have needed help,
We didn't travel far.

## My Pal Bonnie

I was a famous boxer dog,
My colour it was brindle,
And when we went into the woods
A forest fire I'd kindle.

I was not known for my good looks,
I'd frighten most away,
But should I meet a friendly type
I'd do my best to stay.

I lick when told, I'd rather bite
When strangers come to stay;
If nothing else, it helps to keep
Unwelcome ones away.

Our boss is kind and full of vim,
For he knows we'd die for him,
So rid yourself of all your fears;
Whilst we're on guard, there are no tears.

We love our Bonnie like a son,
For after all is said and done,
A doggy's life and all it takes,
We overlook his small mistakes.

## *Trees*

Earth's largest, living,
Breathing thing.
Spirit of Creation,
Held in trust,
By every nation.

Proud head in skies
Aloft – but not aloof –
For once
Let's realise
Nature's perfection.

Host to all things,
A haven at night –
Squirrels and termites,
Robins and spiders,
And weirdies on wing.

Lovers' hurried, whispered,
Entreating pleas.
Trysting secrets
For none – but
Trees.

Roots,
Playfully undermining –
Waving flora.
Roots mischievously chasing
Subterranean fauna.

Thor and friends,
Relentless reapers – leave
Verdant mantle stripped,
To covering bark –
Quite stark.

The annual round,
You choose
Which of these brilliant hues,
'Ere in one flash of autumn gold
Fade darkly.

Majestic sentinel – ignored;
Leafed arms with frantic warning send;
Unheeding mortal plots,
Marine beginning
To cataclysmic end.

Bough breaks, falls,
Dead, buried, deeply,
Waits aeons' call
To earthly flame,
And dies again.

## *The Best Things in Life*

I think of things I used to like,
It was from the age of three,
And much to my amazement
I found it all was free!

And so through life I found the same
In things that could please me,
I never had to bargain things,
For the best things in life are free.

So should you meet a stranger
Not knowing where to go,
The cost cannot be measured
To tell him what you know.

We will be always arguing
On how much things have cost,
But never stop to ponder
On how much we have lost.

The saying goes we arrived with nought,
Will go the same old way,
So make the most of what we have
And most of our short stay.

## *Have You Seen Our Beggar?*

Have you seen our beggar
Who lives down our main street?
He's dressed up like an old rag doll
With no shoes on his feet.

Sometimes he brings his dog along,
Who looks as sad as he,
But both look well upon their face –
'Tis a mystery to me.

They both will squat in shelter from the rain,
His hat upon the ground
Against a little written note
Which asks you for your pound.

As with most days came the end,
Of this they had no choice,
So up they jumped and off they went
Secure in their Rolls-Royce.

So when you pity others
Who just hang around the town,
Be sure your facts are always right
Before you run them down!

# *Conversation*

I sweat
And strain
And find
Great consternation
For my relief
I should have sought belief
In conversation
We will find,
Like other kind,
The answer to salvation,
So if we're meek
We learn to speak
This conversation.
In this life
We may find strife
As well as jubilation,
But we will find
Our peace of mind
If we try conversation;
We will find
That folk are kind
Forget their celebration
If you just ask them
If they'll try
To use this conversation.

## A Sailor's Life

A sailor's life was for me
So I could sail upon the sea;
The sharks could eat where they thought best
If they didn't eat my green string vest.

The sails went up and touched the sky
And waved at seagulls passing by,
But when they saw our friendly puss,
Didn't mind what they dropped on us.

Sometimes the weather got quite rough,
But we were made of sterner stuff
And when the wavecrests reached quite high,
Not only would our brave hearts die.

So cargo's dropped, the voyage over,
A welcome sight the cliffs of Dover;
We see the sights and drink like men
Then off we'll go to sea again.

Fellow maidens please beware;
Fall in love but have a care;
He likes the sea, oh this is true,
But will he fall in love with you?

## The Roly Polys

It turned out such a sunny day,
The raindrops they were few,
So we donned the proper garb
And off we went to Crewe.

In Crewe we found a theatre
With seats in the front row;
The cast was of a music hall
And five girls whom you know.

We really liked the singers
And the conjurer with his son;
Best of all we loved the girls
Before the show began.

There were just the five of them
Who cared not for their weight,
And when they danced the taps rang out
And made the floor vibrate.

The RPs they were wonderful
Their taps and songs were swell
And should they come to Nantwich town
Sure I'll be there as well.

## *The Fairy on the Christmas Tree*

She's seen so many things before
Dropped right beneath her tree,
The postie is our Santa Claus
Who delivers things to me.

Each year the prices increase
From where they first began,
When all we got were bags of sweets
And ate them to a man.

But times have changed and so have we
Since we played with our shooters;
The sweeties too have gone amiss
Now we play with computers.

The Christmas cards had Christmas scenes
To say what it's about;
Let's remember good old days
Where there's no need to shout.

But today we give them loads
Of things we never had,
But let's be honest and admit
It wasn't all the bad.

## Remember the Robin

Remember, he's our feathered friend
In spite of all his bobbin';
He stays with us throughout the year,
He is our Mr Robin.

At times his food is buried
By snow upon the ground;
Now is the time for you to help
And spread his food around.

Let's not forget the young ones
Who come along each year,
If they haven't flown by Christmas,
They have so much to fear.

Our Robin lends his likeness
On cards we all must buy
To show we still remember
The folk who've said, 'Goodbye.'

Let's thank the bird and all his young
For what they've done for us;
Let's make sure they're all well fed
And do not make a fuss.

## Words

I try to write some poetry,
The words get in a ruck
But when I try to make them rhyme,
That's when I'm really stuck.

Not that I'm too thick
To put my thoughts on paper,
At noughts and crosses I'm the champ
And all that sort of caper.

The trouble is I think too hard
And tenses seem to beat me;
The future has already gone,
It passed by oh so sweetly.

The vowels make such a dreadful sound,
They know just where to go;
The five of them each makes a word,
As only I should know.

And so I think I'll start again,
So plain except to me;
And so I think I'll go right back
And learn my two times three.

## The Burglar

His footsteps sneaked across the grass,
He did not make a sound;
He chose the quietest door there was
So he did not have to pound.

And so the sorry tale went on,
The houses robbed were many;
Some who thought their homes immune
Were left without a penny.

Sometimes he took to stealing cars,
Regardless of miles upon the clocks,
And he said, 'You'd be amazed
How many folk leave keys in locks.'

The police have done their very best
To stop the thieving of our stuff;
The thieves say they won't strike again,
But are the terms quite long enough?

But time, and time alone will tell;
Does trust make thieves revert?
Or at the thought of being good
Like squaddies, do they desert?

## *My Garden*

You're nearer to God's heart in a garden
 Than anywhere else on earth,
 But forget all the heartache in digging
And perspiring for all you are worth.

I really don't mind all the digging,
The exercise is good for me;
Apart from the beauty the flowers display,
The garden's great to see.

The bluebells come every springtime,
The daffodils spread just as well;
Don't know of the pH factor,
Or some that are too long to tell.

I find there is peace in the garden,
No noises or rows to intrude;
The flowers will grow, but the ground must be damp,
To show the rain has endured.

And so I escape to my garden
As I have done in the past;
I pray that the future is kind to me
And makes all my visits last.

## No Trading

But Christ, he wore a worried look
As down the street he strode,
The synagogues were built for prayer,
Or so he had been told.

He heard the dreadful sound again
That crashed upon his ear,
The sound of men creating trade
And things he should not hear.

The men were in the synagogue
And in the loaning trade;
They lent you any sort of money,
But you paid a higher rate.

Anxious to put all things right
And tired of the whole affair,
He dumped the tables and the men
And every single chair.

The men protested at this deed
In voices loud and clear,
But he stood firm and told them all,
There is no trading here.

## The Angel

The angel dived and then he swerved,
His wingtips touched a cloud,
'I'd better do what I've been told
And investigate the crowd.'

So watching that he did not crash,
He landed on the earth;
He did not know which way to turn,
But read for all he was worth.

One sign read, 'To London Town',
The place he had to go,
He didn't mind the distance,
The locals he would know.

The visit was a shock to him –
Five hundred years had passed,
The houses and the people changed –
Would nothing ever last?

He noticed that the people cared
More than years ago;
They cared for pets and many things
And this was nice to know.

## Santune

Santune, O Santune, how my heart
Will remember thee.
Your ever-open door for all
Who face adversity.

Even in the stillness of the
Darkest night,
My ever-waiting button plays guardian
Till the change to light.

When the world deserts us,
We thought we knew best.
Santune sends its friendly welcome –
Come, friend, come and rest.

So I arrived at Santune's steps,
Lonely, frightened and just a little fearful.
And ask, 'What now, what now?'
In a voice that's just a little tearful.

What is the secret of this everlasting
Search for health?
Simply put all your faith
In God, Santune, and of course, yourself.

## *Fishing*

I saw her laughing, smiling face,
I saw what I could catch;
I picked my pitch an hour ago,
It was a fishing match.

Each time I went to sling my hook,
I saw her smiling face.
I caught the largest rainbow trout,
My price was no disgrace.

Some who said they'd caught a lot,
Made for the nearest shop.
They bought the biggest fish they saw,
So their wives them wouldn't chop.

I saw the smiling girl again,
On my way to adult school.
I did not let her see my face –
I was not a fool.

The following years sped quickly by,
As they so often do.
She should be quite grown up by now,
For she was only two.

## *11 November, Lest We Forget*

Lest we forget the brave ones
Who led the first attack,
We must still remember
That they never will come back.

The wars, they cover everyone,
Soldiers and civilians, too;
Let's give our thanks to all of them,
That's what we will do.

Some folk, we can't forget them;
Time passes, it is true,
Let us say a simple prayer,
That's what we all must do.

Whoever wants to start a war,
It's neither you nor me;
Each one thinks that he is right,
Youth backs this tragedy.

Can we learn from history
The folly of our ways?
And know that Jesus Christ alone
Will give us happier days.

## *If Jesus…*

If Jesus came to earth again,
Would he be proud of us?
No time to talk, or even smile.
While queuing for our bus.

In life he owned but little,
He started in a shed,
It takes a lifetime now to pay
For a roof above our head.

Status symbols now hold sway
(We want the world to know),
He didn't need eight cylinders
To bolster his ego.

The world is still a wondrous place –
Green fields, wild birds and water,
But now beneath the constant threat
Of encroaching bricks and mortar.

If Jesus came to earth again,
Would he just stand and stare,
Compare the shores of Galilee
With the lights of Leicester Square?

Near on two thousand years to gain
Our own eternity –
We chose to spend these years in strife;
Is that our destiny?

No need to come to earth again,
Just let us get this right;
Whene'er we feel the need of him,
He's there – both day and night.

This world of ours yields plenty,
Enough to eat and drink.
Yet half the world's in poverty,
It really makes you think.

A million billion pounds to put
Our watchdogs in the sky,
One tiny little part would save
So many doomed to die.

So when Jesus comes a-knocking,
And we hear him o'er the din,
It may well be the world's last chance
To say, 'Oh, please come in!'

## *Fire*

The fireman climbed the escape steps
Till he nearly reached the sky.
The smoke had almost touched the clouds,
Because the flames had grown so high.

He thought about the crowd below,
Some caught up in the fire,
His hope was that he'd get them out,
It was all he could desire.

As he saw the scene below,
A building wrapped in flame,
He thought he'd get a safer job –
Lion taming was his aim.

He thought of all the damage
The smallest flame could do,
Then the water from his hosepipe
Would soak things through and through.

If people were more careful,
And safety plans could hatch.
If they could see the damage,
Caused by a simple match.

## *The Last Supper*

Would Jesus say the same today?
 'Leave your nets and family –
I've found a place where we can eat
Because you twelve will dine with me.'

Perhaps we've changed from bread and wine
Though symbolic of his blood.
We are offered tastier food,
A chance to make them all feel good.

Christ told them that his end was near,
And ways they could remember him;
He said that one would let him down,
That's when their faces looked quite grim.

The cockerel crowed, as he had said,
Its call was loud and clear;
The third call made him heavenly frown,
He knew the end was near.

The twelve men who had gathered there
Swore that he should wear a crown;
But fate decided otherwise,
For one had let him down.

## Nine, Ten, Out

I drove quickly down the jagged drive,
And drove at such a pace.
My pride it was the four-in-hand,
I swore 'twould win this race.

This was just a small town show,
Where horses make the grade.
They then go on to bigger towns,
That's how our champs are made.

And so we fought our way through rounds,
Pushed on towards the top.
Just one more single step to take,
That's why we mustn't stop.

And what a day the final was,
We started with their cheer.
And as we reached the winning post,
They all reached for their beer.

We reached out for the winner's cup
It all seemed like a joke.
We very nearly grabbed the cup,
But then we all awoke.

## The Early Bird

The cockerel made his morning call,
Woke all the folk around.
The eggs were laid just anywhere
But never on the ground.

The cockerel spied a likely hen,
But had never heard her cluck.
After much examination,
They found she was a duck!

But proud were just a few old hens,
For each were given nests,
But laid their eggs in other homes,
And turned out to be pests.

The hens said they would boycott
All the eggs they laid.
But foxes came and pinched the lot,
So different plans were made.

In time the farmer got fed up,
His costs had gone too high,
He found he made more money
By baking chicken pie!

## A Year Goes By

It's just a single year that's passed
Since first we let her go.
Do we still remember her?
Of this you surely know.

She left a void which can't be filled
By any tools on hand,
No one can ever take her place,
Not any mortal in the land.

What shall we do to count the cost,
Of someone in the land?
Someone we never can replace,
We know you understand.

But life goes on its merry way,
Regardless of the strain.
Let us hope that we have learned enough
To make the future sane.

There comes a time to all of us,
When our loved one now departs.
Let's hope that not a single one
Forgets the Queen of Hearts.

## He Came

He came upon this earth of ours
Near two thousand years ago.
He showed us all the way to live,
And not our wealth to show.

People said that he'd be king,
With fine lands such as Devon.
He would, of course, one day be king,
But in a place called Heaven.

He saved many with his miracles,
That's when he called on God.
His Father was Creator,
To Whom he would just nod.

In three of his short teaching years,
He changed most of mankind.
Some folk believed his serious words,
But many were merely blind.

Did he want King Herod's throne,
Armies in bright array?
He gave his life to prove his point,
I hope we meet some day.

## What is in a Name?

Which of the characters in time,
Thrills us and warms our blood?
He robbed the rich to feed the poor,
His name was Robin Hood.

Perhaps you are a climber,
The mountains thrill you still.
They searched the hill for water,
Were known as Jack and Jill.

Perhaps you like the royal queen,
Who lives in London town,
And just like our own pussy cat,
You tried to track her down.

Or there is the open sea,
And the life afloat.
Meet the owl and pussycat,
In their sweet little pea green boat.

Snow White met her little men,
Who obeyed every spoken command.
But if you like another one,
There are many in the land.

## Sarah's Find

I first saw my dream house
In Wrenbury one day,
A piece of nature's wonderland;
That's where I'm going to stay.

We have to get the roses
That grow around the door,
And make sure that no buttercups,
Ever peep above the floor.

But what about the kitchen?
Will it be adequate?
Or will it prove to be too small?
A point I deprecate.

But we must work so very hard,
Never from our path must roam,
To make this great big pile of bricks
Into our family home.

But life has many pitfalls,
Of this you all must know.
And when the going gets too tough,
We have a place to go.

## *Jesus*

What were his thoughts upon the cross,
Gazing at the multitude?
They jeered and mocked, but all admired,
His everlasting fortitude.

He spent his life to save mankind,
Whatever they had done.
He knew it would take his life,
From when it had begun.

He knew there was another world,
Where his Father reigned,
To go there was an earthly claim,
But first His Will must be obtained.

He chose a dozen followers,
Who were God-fearing men.
They thought that he had left for good,
But then he rose again.

But what about an after-life,
With joy for evermore?
We hope that God will guide us right,
And steer us to that heavenly shore.

# Going Racing

Inside a row of starting gates,
A row of horses stood.
A pistol fired the long awaited 'Off!'
The horses kicked up many streams of mud.

A lady screamed because she thought,
She'd lost her little smalls.
We had to call the horses back,
For some had raced inside the stalls.

Two mares led the first half race,
With Fireworks far behind.
But Caterpillar reduced his ten length lead,
To show that he was kind.

The rain came down so very hard
And turned the course to mud.
Some got a lift on ferryboats,
And lifeboats if they could.

They tried to swim, but found it hard,
They had not got the strength.
But Birdseye came up on the left,
And won by just a length.

## *The Dining Room*

The dining room was empty,
They all had had their fill;
They took their pills for various ills,
Then disregarded the bill.

Most would eat what Dave supplied,
It was of course the best;
To satisfy the multitude,
Must put him to the test.

All in all we don't do bad
With choices for our meal,
So thanks to Dave and all his staff,
For what he does reveal.

Asparagus or lettuce leaves,
They all go down the same;
If they fail to take that route,
There's no one here to blame.

And so we eat our merry way,
In spite of what they say,
And if the carrots won't go down,
They just will have to stay.

## Only a Mouse

When I was young, I thought I'd be
As big as any house,
But fate decided otherwise,
And I ended up a mouse.

I quickly learned what to avoid,
From Mum, who shared the mat;
First of all was pussy,
Better known as cat.

My best friend was the budgie,
Entrapped there in a cage,
But whenever I got near to him,
He flew into a rage.

I would eat almost anything,
When offered I would please,
But best of all, I did enjoy,
A simple piece of cheese.

The entrance to my castle
Was a tiny little hole,
Through which none could pass,
Unless tiny, like a vole.

# The New Brother

(Five-minute sketch especially written for 'Musical Sounds')

## LIST OF CHARACTERS

SARAH, about 16 years old
ANGIE, Sarah's sister, about 8 years old
JEAN, a friend, about 15 years old
DANNY, about 16 years old

## A STREET CORNER IN WINTER

| | |
|---|---|
| ANGIE: | Sarah, I'm cold… Ooh, and my fingers, they're ever so frozen. |
| SARAH: | Serves you right. |
| ANGIE: | Ooh… Why? |
| SARAH: | Five pairs of gloves you've had since Christmas – and lost them! |
| ANGIE: | Not my fault – I forget where I put them. |
| SARAH: | Never mind, we'll write to Santa again. Oh look, here comes Jean. |

*Jean approaches, muffled up, smiling.*

| | |
|---|---|
| JEAN: | Hello, you two. |

| SARAH: | Hello, Jean. |
| JEAN: | What on earth are you hanging about for in this weather? |

*Sarah fidgets.*

| SARAH: | Uhm... Well... We're waiting... |
| JEAN: | I can see that, but what for? |
| SARAH: | Well... we're waiting... for... |
| JEAN: | Good heavens, what's the great mystery? |
| SARAH: | We're waiting for... for my brother. |
| JEAN: | Brother! But you haven't got a brother. |
| SARAH: | Not yet, no. [*She hesitates*] But I soon will have. |
| JEAN: | Soon? You mean your mother's had a baby? |
| SARAH: | No. |
| JEAN: | You mean a kind of instant brother? |
| SARAH: | Yes, you could call him that. We're waiting for Mum and Dad. They've gone to fetch... Well, to bring... Anyway, they've gone to the orphanage. |
| JEAN: | Oh, I see. Oh, that's smashing! Hear that, Angie? You're going to have a brother. |
| ANGIE: | Ugh! I hate boys, and... I'm cold. |

*Angie looks puzzled and mumbles to herself, while Danny approaches. When he sees the girls, he gives a few wolf whistles.*

| JEAN: | Here comes that boy you're very keen on, Sarah. |
| SARAH: | I *am not*! I hate him. |
| JEAN: | Then why are you blushing? |
| DANNY: | Hello, girls. What's all this, then? A mother's meeting? |
| JEAN: | Oh, you can't have heard then? |

| | |
|---|---|
| DANNY: | Heard what? |
| JEAN: | Sarah and Angie are going to have a young brother today. |
| DANNY: | [*He is silent for a moment*] Oh, that's really great. Has your mother had a baby? |
| ANGIE: | [*She looks up at Sarah*] What's an orphanage, Sarah? |
| SARAH: | Well... it's a... |
| DANNY: | [*Interrupting*] It's a kind of second home, for children who haven't got a mum and dad. |
| ANGIE: | But everybody's got a mum and dad! |
| JEAN: | Well, they certainly started out with them. |
| ANGIE: | What happened? |
| DANNY: | It's not easy to explain, Angie. |
| ANGIE: | Please try and explain... I want to know. |
| DANNY: | Well, sometimes their parents have died and gone to heaven. And sometimes... sometimes they have split up, gone their separate ways. And left their children all alone. |
| ANGIE: | All alone, and lonely? Why that's awful! |
| SARAH: | True, but it's not only children who can be lonely. |
| JEAN: | What do you mean? |
| SARAH: | Why, some of the old folk are lonely. Like Mrs Brownsword down the road, and Mrs Wilding on the other side. I'm sure they're lonely. |
| JEAN: | Yes, I've seen Mrs Brownsword hobbling to the shops at the weekend; she has rheumatism, and never complains or asks for help. |
| DANNY: | And we never offer to help, do we? |

| JEAN: | But Mrs Wilding is quite fit, isn't she? Why doesn't she join a club or something? |
|---|---|
| DANNY: | It's not as easy as that. |
| JEAN: | Well, there are lots of clubs about for them... And all free. There's the Darby and Joan club. |
| DANNY: | Quite true, but many old people are weary and shy... You know, mentally tired. They need that extra little bit of encouragement. |
| SARAH: | You mean a really friendly welcome? |
| DANNY: | Yes, it's so easy to feel unwanted when you're old, and for that matter when you're very young, too. |
| SARAH: | You know, I've never heard you talk like this before, Danny. |
| DANNY: | Well, I understand their feelings. You see, girls, I was brought up in that orphanage... Must be off now. It's been nice seeing you again. Bye, girls. |
| ANGIE: | Bye, Danny. |

*Sarah and Jean stare at each other in open-mouthed silence for a moment.*

| SARAH: | Well I never! Danny an orphan! |
|---|---|
| JEAN: | Sarah, are you thinking what I'm thinking? I mean, about helping the old folk when we can? |
| SARAH: | Yes I am, Jean. From now on we must help them wherever possible, and I'm sure Angie will help, as well. |
| ANGIE: | Ooooer, yes! I'm ever so good at helping. |

*[Jean and Sarah smile at Angie]*

| JEAN: | Look, Sarah, look! Your mum and dad! [*She points*] They're coming up the street! |
|---|---|
| SARAH: | Where? Oh yes, I can see them now. |
| JEAN: | They've got a little boy with them! |

| | |
|---|---|
| ANGIE: | A little boy? How old is he? |
| SARAH: | He looks a little younger than you. |
| ANGIE: | [*Very interested now*] How big is he? |
| SARAH: | Not quite as big as you are, dear, but why? |
| ANGIE: | Shall I be able to bash him, when he's naughty? |
| SARAH: | [*Laughing*] Oh, you little horror! Come on, all of you. Let's go and meet my new brother. |

*They dash off, excitedly shouting 'Mum' and 'Dad'.*

# Spring

Daffodils show that spring is near,
Most bees swarm – they have no fear.
Rabbits gallop in the grass,
There's no stream they will not pass.

We get a warning every day
That our spring is on its way.
The buds have stopped their winter toil,
And now will peep above the soil.

The young birds must learn how to fly,
So they can vanish in the sky.
The worms will grope their way around,
As they burrow in the ground.

Young ones in the nearby zoo
Know exactly what to do.
Visitors admire their childish charm,
Hope they never take to harm.

Nature tends the young quite well,
Their secrets it will never tell.
Their future is our greatest gem,
If only we look after them.

## *He'll Return*

He'll return to earth one day,
Then it's too late to start to pray.
We're judged by all the things we've done,
Ever since our lives began.

We read that Jesus loved us all,
Though in his life bad things befell.
He helped the crippled end their strife,
So, in thanks, we took his life.

His people said he would be king,
But not on earth, was his thinking.
Three short years was all he had
To change the world to good from bad.

Disciples backed him most of the time,
Till Romans charged our Lord with crime.
In course of time Jesus was sold,
For a few paltry pieces of gold.

Although we think we're very good,
We all have times we reach the mud.
Let's hope that everyone will find
That our God is just and kind.

## The Boy

The boy stood on the burning deck,
His clothing all in tatters.
He kept his cool and long john pants,
That was all that mattered.

The boat had struck a north-west storm,
And lost most of her sail.
All the mice had learned to swim,
Could withstand any gale.

The skipper did not mind the storm,
Said it would do some good.
So he marched right to the poop-deck,
Though plastered all in mud.

The passing ships all hailed him,
Thought it was a great big joke.
And when the stern blew off the boat,
Said it was a master stroke.

The boat sailed on throughout the night,
Past piles of looted junk.
Then all at once the keel fell off,
Then our trim craft was sunk.

## *Jesus Christ*

Hail him, our one and only saviour,
Through him may we our sins atone.
We need his strength and all his glory,
We cannot do it on our own.

The Jews expected vast great armies,
Of which he'd be their finest king.
To which he showed no great attraction,
But pursued his lonely wandering.

His questions caused them great distress,
He wanted them to know
His Father's home for all mankind,
If humility they'd show.

But life took on a different turn,
As it often will.
They accused him of heinous ambitions,
He never could fulfil.

He wanted just a quiet world,
Where men would live in peace.
Neighbours would be our closest friends,
And love would never cease.

## I Visit Church House

I went along to our Church House,
They say it is so nice.
I never saw an earwig,
Nor did I see those mice.

I feel so very guilty,
For Mum has been so kind.
So now I want the sweetest home,
The best that I can find.

I need not have been so worried,
As I walked round the ground.
I could have searched for evermore,
And no better could have found.

The patients they were waited on,
By a very devoted staff.
Who always worked so very hard,
But found the time to laugh.

We all will need a helping hand,
When old age comes along.
But let us be like Mother,
And meet life with a song.

## The Beauty Queen

She was the cutest, brightest girl
That I have ever seen,
And dressed up in the proper clothes
She'd be a beauty queen.

I caught her loving smile one day
When I went for a walk;
I wondered if my heart would jump
If we should ever talk.

I often built large sandcastles
On trips quite near the sea,
But thought they were not grand enough
To house both her and me.

I tried to glimpse her many times
As I passed by her way.
My walks were quite intentional,
Though no sight on any day.

I treasure all these memories
That happened just to me.
By now she should be quite grown up
For she was only three.

## Diana

This girl died as she had lived
And gave the sick some hope.
And though they thought they'd had their lot,
She showed that they could cope.

She may have been our righteous Queen,
But now we'll never know
We only have fond memories,
Before we let her go.

She had a very good night out,
Before her fateful end.
And took her loved one with her too,
Wherever God might send.

The good she did will still live on,
For sick and well the same.
Remember that disease will come,
And no one is to blame.

So where do we go on from here?
Thank God for her short life.
That we may learn from what she did.
And rid ourselves of strife.

## Night-time

I gazed at the horizon,
The sun was but a frame.
The moon was bright and spread its light
Until the morning came.

The owls were in their element,
I heard their tu-whit tu-whoo.
The bunnies left their rabbit holes,
They knew just what to do.

The bats had left the belfry,
They didn't need their eyes.
They jumped upon the passing moths,
Oh, what a great surprise!

Many things come out at night
To scavenge for their food.
But many find on their return,
They have a different brood.

They said that it was safe at night,
To do their steady round.
But just who we might meet at night,
It makes your poor heart pound.

## The Beggar Man

I looked upon the beggar man,
Who lay down in the street.
I'd seen all kinds of wondrous things,
But never this to meet

He did not have a house at all,
Somewhere to lay his head.
The pavement was his pillow,
The bare road was his bed.

Someone there just had to help,
Give refuge from mankind,
But who would give this man some help
Or aid of any kind?

We think about Samaritans,
When they went for a ride.
Would they stop to help this man,
Or seek the other side?

This is where we first came in –
Does your pride unbend?
Do you really try to make
Your enemy your friend?

## The Colour Bar

I used to have a colour bar
Many years ago.
You need to have a white skin,
A skin as white as snow.

One day our lovely house caught fire,
But why we did not know.
The blaze soon brought the neighbours out
From houses in the row.

The fire soon spread about the house
Up to the very top floor.
I was trapped in my bedroom,
I could not see the door.

Our local coalman was about
Delivering bags of coal;
He pulled me from that blazing house,
May God preserve his soul!

We had to bath and clean our clothes,
After this setback.
The coalman also had a bath,
But his skin was still as black.

## Never Too Late

I was behind those prison bars
For things that I had done;
I tried to keep to prison rules,
But it was not fun.

I thought about the many years
My freedom was denied.
They said that I must speak the truth,
But every time I lied.

It seemed that this would be my life;
I'd spend my lifetime there.
One day someone left a book,
Told how our Christ did fare.

This proved to be a turning point
With every page I read.
I lent the book to all my friends,
Christianity soon spread.

And so my life began again
Upon my discharge date,
But one thing must I say to you,
It never is too late.

## Tribute to our Stan

Just a word about our Stan,
He was the city's favourite man.
Football was his major game –
To him, all sports were just the same.

He started at an early age,
But soon became the nation's rage.
He dribbled past a host of men
And soon approached the lion's den.

Cautionary words were never used,
Opponents never were abused;
Always he played the best he can,
Was nature's perfect gentleman.

Now he has gone, but left his mark
For which, with thanks, we all remark.
Can we hope to match his style?
Would make our living here worthwhile.

We think about a statuette
For this man we can't forget.
Now I think we'll make a start,
We'll always keep him, in our heart.

## Worth the Wait

It happens every waking day –
An anxious girl gives birth;
The grim faces of our duty staff
Show there's no time for mirth.

Her mind went back to nine hard months
When his face was just a blob,
But now she felt she must prepare
To do a lifetime job.

Her life would never be the same
When young one came along;
Will nappies alter her sweet life?
And it won't be to a song.

But don't forget you have a name
Upon the family tree;
Also, the most important thing,
You're now a family.

So now as you await the time,
(Gets nearer to the day),
The nurses and the doctors there
Will see that you're okay!

## The Lottery

If I had won the lottery,
How happy I should be.
I think I'd buy the finest house,
Then I would plant a tree.

Perhaps I'd plan my holidays,
Around the world I'd go,
See Egypt's ancient pyramids,
Iceland's expanse of snow.

Then come relatives and friends,
I'd help them on their way;
They'd have the finest of hotels,
That's where they'd have to stay.

Next we have the homeless kids
Who struggle up the hill;
Perhaps they think that life's a joke,
Perhaps they always will.

Money pays for all those things
On which our life depends,
But one thing that it cannot do,
It can't bring back old friends.

## *Born Again*

I give my life to Jesus Christ,
Who died to save us all.
Be he prince or beggar man,
No one's beyond recall.

We may have marred our earthly life,
By deeds we can't repeat.
Now is the time to start again,
He'll put us on our feet.

He gave us our forgiveness,
Forgets about the past.
But we must keep the promise,
That our faithfulness will last.

Then we start our life again,
But on the other side.
Everyone is equal,
And has no need of pride.

We'll meet with ones whom we had lost
So many years ago.
We may also meet the Lord,
The Bible tells us so.

## *Who?*

Who made the famous butterfly,
And humming busy bee?
Who made the tallest living thing?
I mean, of course, the tree.

This covers all of living things,
Though changes come and go.
Some grow in the fiercest heat,
While some live in the snow.

'Tis said we are aquatic things,
Life started in the sea.
It may or may not be quite true,
In time we hope that we shall see.

It is just two thousand years,
Since Jesus Christ first came.
We have a lifetime to decide
That our faith is still the same.

You may decide to give your faith
To one who gave his life.
And that it's far far better
Than ending it in strife.

## Who Never Asked

There is this one we shall not name
Who never asked for earthly fame,
But though so many years have passed,
His memory will always last.

One day we had to make a choice
And spoke with a resounding voice.
Throughout our lifetime we must tell
It was our sweet Immanuel.

His Father said he should begin
By saving all the world from sin,
Ignoring all the local strife,
The Son gave up his earthly life.

He left a list of his commands
That answered all the world's demands.
We only have but ten of these,
Which we should learn with ease.

Our doubts upon the fire we burn
Hoping for his quick return;
He showed us how we should treat death
Before he drew his final breath.

## The Boy Stood on the Burning Deck

The boy stood on the burning deck,
His shoes were made of rubber,
And as the flames licked round his feet,
The boy began to blubber.

And so it was with all the crew,
They blew up one by one;
The mice queued up to swim ashore,
The crew, they all had gone!

It started all quite so small,
The crew had played with matches,
So for their pains they got no gold
Nor mention in despatches.

The boat and sails were well ablaze
As seen both far and near,
And when at last the keel went down
No one was heard to cheer.

So just remember when you play,
There's no one there to blame;
Except to know a little spark
Will quickly turn to flame.

## *For the Boss*

Pretty little fellow,
Mighty like a rose,
Don't know what to call him,
But we think he's one of those.

## Fairies in my Garden

There are fairies in my garden,
They are there most every night,
They twist and dance their pirouettes,
To everyone's delight.

The skylarks form the chorus,
Complete in every round,
They've kept time for centuries,
To help friends on the ground.

The fairies line up in their twos,
Prepare for their next figure,
So helped by many garden friends,
Their numbers soon grow bigger.

All through the long hours of the night
They dance, lit by the moonbeams,
Helped by stoat and weasel folk,
Avoided the wrath of trout streams.

When morning light creeps into view,
It is the ending of their show,
Some creep or fly or mostly walk,
To homes that only they would know.

## Years Ago

It must have been a great time,
All those years ago,
When Christ spelled out his message,
That our forebears had to know.

The roof creaked as they lowered him down,
Dead, he could not talk,
But Jesus quietly said to him,
'Take up thy bed and walk.'

Many things he showed them
When they sat down to dine,
They found few fish most adequate,
And turned water into wine.

The ocean waves had trapped them,
Their time had come they knew,
But Christ held back the torrid sea,
And they filed quietly through.

Miracles happen all the time,
If only we could see,
The Lord moves in a mysterious way,
It could be you or me!

## Physiotherapists, Thank You!

Was it only yesterday
I first rolled down that corridor of hope?
Was it only yesterday
I thought walking, running, jumping are just a joke?

A joke where no one laughed, but stared
Or glared at our immobility,
And left angels with physio blouses
To clear up frail and helpless humanity.

So life takes on another turning
And questions all those things we did not do.
So stop the clock – hold Father Time,
And let our dearest hopes and dreams come true!

'Stop your dreaming – lots to do,'
Says Julie in her no nonsense voice.
'We'll do our part – you must, too!'
Upon reflection, there's simply no choice.

So months of bend and stretch and pull,
No chance of any shirking –
When suddenly a finger moves –
My God, this treatment's working!

## My Sister's Birthday

My sister gazed at all her cards
Ranged in every room.
No one had forgotten her,
All had split the gloom.

What shall we get for her birthday?
No one seemed to know.
We could get a nice puppy,
But puppies seem to grow.

Tennis can be quite a game
It helps to keep you fit,
But what about the breakages
And windows we might hit?

We decided on a baby doll,
Within her own brown box,
The lid was simply fastened down,
But there were not any locks.

So there she sat, two years old
With baby face and golden locks.
She had cast the doll upon the floor,
And was playing with the box!

## *You Want to Dance?*

There comes a time in most our lives,
When we feel the need to dance!
This could lead to two left feet,
Or simply to romance.

First we place our left foot,
Followed by our right,
If we get in someone's way,
It may end with a bite.

The dances are all different,
The steps are different too.
We have to be so careful,
And act like Fu Man Chu.

Music sometimes takes the lead,
Like Strauss's engrossing *Blue Danube*
You hum it all the way to work,
In the evening, on the tube.

When you decide to take a step,
A new world opens up for you.
Should you trot or should you waltz?
It doesn't matter what you do.